Quizzes for Kids

Quizzes for Kids

Quizzes to Stimulate Thinking in Young People Aged 10–16

Tom Trifonoff

Copyright © 2017 by Tom Trifonoff.

ISBN:	Softcover	978-1-5434-0416-6
	eBook	978-1-5434-0415-9

All rights reserved. No part of this book may be reproduced or transmitted in any form or by any means, electronic or mechanical, including photocopying, recording, or by any information storage and retrieval system, without permission in writing from the copyright owner.

Any people depicted in stock imagery provided by Thinkstock are models, and such images are being used for illustrative purposes only.
Certain stock imagery © Thinkstock.

Print information available on the last page.

Rev. date: 09/30/2017

To order additional copies of this book, contact:
Xlibris
1-800-455-039
www.Xlibris.com.au
Orders@Xlibris.com.au
768276

Introduction

While there are many books out there covering quizzes for adults in a variety of ways, either through the Pub Quiz or Quiz Night format, or just questions to fire at adults to see how knowledgeable they are, there are very few books for younger people.

In an age where young people can access information at the click of a button, there is very little to see how much they actually know and remember. That is the reason behind this book. As a teacher for over 30 years, I found that young people like to be challenged on a variety of topics. When I conducted quizzes at school, I found that their competitive spirit and the challenge of getting a correct answer were just as strong as any adult. It also highlighted their teamwork as a group member; again it was a microcosm of an adult team in exactly the same situation.

Kids are eager to learn and retain information. This book, **Quizzes For Kids** is the perfect situation where they can see how much they do actually retain. As with adults, every person has a favourite category, and they will do better with some questions rather than others. This is where being in a team will bring out the best in everyone. Each quiz round features a wide variety of questions over numerous topics to cater for the whole group. While it will be easy to have rounds of quizzes on specific topics, e.g., sport, history, geography etc., this can put some kids off straight away. They may not be strong on sports questions, so that round will be very unsatisfying to them, and they may switch off. The rounds of quizzes in this book have a variety of topics in each one of them-some sport, history, entertainment etc. to make up the 25 questions in each round.

There are also answer sheets provided at the end of the book which can be photocopied for use. There are two types of answer sheets, one for a team and one for individuals, depending on how the quiz master wants to run the quiz. Answers to each quiz are provided on the next page.

All the questions to the quizzes are different-500 DIFFERENT questions. It's easy to get lazy and reword a question that covers the same topic. That doesn't happen in this book.

The quizzes can be run on a formal basis, ie, setting up of teams; kids playing the quiz individually; or just firing questions to the kids on a random basis. If you decide to use teams, a suggestion would be of no more than 5 in a team. That worked best when I ran my quizzes in school. Teams of 2, 3 and 4 are can also be quite effective.

I hope that the questions in the book are stimulating, challenging and fun and that at the end of it all the participants have enjoyed it and learnt something about their world at the same time.

Tom Trifonoff

October 2017

Quiz One

1. Who had an encounter with the three bears?
2. What is the name given to an animal that only eats plants?
3. Which liner sank on her maiden voyage in 1912?
4. In area, what is Australia's largest state?
5. In what year did Barack Obama become President of the USA?
6. In netball, what position do the letters GD indicate?
7. What is the largest country in South America?
8. What TV series is set in Summer Bay?
9. What breed of dog is Goofy-a basset hound, spaniel or bloodhound?
10. What is the highest mountain in Australia?
11. In the bible, how many wise men visited the infant Jesus?
12. In which year did World War Two end?
13. Which team won the 2016 World Series of baseball?
14. What is the name of the Australian women's hockey team called?
15. What language gave us such words as stampede, avocado and bonanza?
16. Which is the only animated Pixar movie to include a live-action piece?
17. Which Country is home to half the world's 100 highest bridges? China, USA or Russia?
18. In which year did Coca Cola launch their first recyclable plastic bottle? 1978, 1988 or 1998?
19. Does the name "coyote" (an Aztec word) mean 'wild', 'proud' or 'trickster'?
20. Rome has never hosted the Summer Olympic Games. True or False?
21. What was the Indian city of Mumbai formerly known as-Calcutta, Bombay or Madras?
22. Which way is a television's screen size measured?
23. Which film is the song Ding Dong the Witch is Dead from-Snow White & the Seven Dwarfs, The Wizard of Oz or The Witches?
24. Where was the 2010 FIFA World Cup held-Spain, South Africa or Sweden?
25. What is the capital of Canada?

Answers

1) Goldilocks
2) Herbivores
3) Titanic
4) Western Australia
5) 2008
6) Goal defence
7) Brazil
8) Home and Away
9) Bloodhound
10) Mount Kosciusko
11) Three
12) 1945
13) Chicago Cubs
14) Hockeyroos
15) Spanish
16) WALL-E
17) China
18) 1978
19) Trickster
20) False
21) Bombay
22) Diagonally
23) The Wizard of Oz
24) South Africa
25) Ottawa

Quiz Two

1. What is the name of Winnie the Pooh's donkey friend?
2. What are the three primary colours?
3. Which people travelled in longships and raided Britain from Scandinavia in early medieval times?
4. Who was the Prime Minister of Australia before Malcolm Turnbull?
5. Times Square is a famous district in which US city?
6. How many polo ponies play on the field at one time-8, 10 or 12?
7. What is the fastest land animal in the world?
8. What is the name of the vehicle in which Scooby Doo and his friends travel?
9. Which of these sports has the highest net-badminton, volleyball or tennis?
10. How many states make up the United States of America?
11. Calais is a port in which country?
12. Who was the first Prime Minister of Australia?
13. How many players from one team are on the field in a rugby league match?
14. Of which state was Thomas Playford a Premier?
15. What was the most important means of transportation by the ancient Egyptians?
16. In 'Finding Nemo', what is Nemo's dad called?
17. The famous Ayers Rock in Australia is made of granite, limestone or sandstone?
18. Ascorbic Acid is another name for which Vitamin? A, B or C?
19. Which country gave us the words 'shampoo' and 'pyjamas'?
20. In which English city would you find the first museum in the world to be opened to the public? Oxford, Cambridge or London?
21. Who was the first woman to fly solo across the Atlantic Ocean-Nancy Bird Walton, Sally Ride or Amelia Earhart?
22. What is the most commonly used word in the English language?
23. On what website can you update your status, post on someone's wall and poke someone?
24. What is the name given to the fourth runner in a relay team-the anchor, bridge or sail?
25. How long did it take for the Titanic to sink-3, 8 or 14 hours?

Answers

1) Eeyore
2) Blue, red, yellow
3) Vikings
4) Tony Abbott
5) New York City
6) 8
7) Cheetah
8) The Mystery Machine
9) Volleyball
10) Fifty
11) France
12) Edmund Barton
13) Thirteen
14) South Australia
15) Boat
16) Marvin
17) Sandstone
18) Vitamin C
19) India
20) Oxford
21) Amelia Earhart
22) The
23) Facebook
24) Anchor
25) 3 hours

Quiz Three

1. Who was created by Geppetto the woodcarver?
2. What is a black mamba?
3. What colour are the benches in the House of Representatives in Parliament?
4. In which state or territory is Rockhampton?
5. In which country is Machu Picchu?
6. What form of martial arts involves throwing an opponent to the floor and holding them there-judo, karate or taekwondo?
7. The song, 'A Whole New World' comes from which animated Disney film?
8. Which stringed instrument is bigger than a violin but smaller than a cello?
9. What musical instrument accompanies a flamenco dancer?
10. What is the capital of Germany?
11. What do American's call autumn?
12. What was built first-the Panama Canal or the Suez Canal?
13. What position in netball do the letters WA stand for?
14. What border divides New South Wales and Victoria?
15. What legendary band was known as The Fab Four?
16. What was the original working title for Wreck-it Ralph? Top Score, Best Score or High Score?
17. In which year did Las Vegas officially become a city? 1911, 1941 or 1971?
18. In which year was the LEGO Company founded? 1932, 1942 or 1952?
19. Which is taller- The Eiffel Tower or The Statue of Liberty?
20. The Statue of Liberty was gifted to the United States by which country?
21. Which city was destroyed by Mt Vesuvius in AD79?
22. What does the RSPCA seek to prevent the cruelty to?
23. In the movie 'Up', who is the boy who knocks on Mr Fredricksen's door?
24. How many points does a tem get for a try in rugby league?
25. What does glockenspiel music sound the most like-bells, drums or rattles?

Answers

1) Pinocchio
2) Snake
3) Green
4) Queensland
5) Peru
6) Judo
7) Aladdin
8) Viola
9) Guitar
10) Berlin
11) Fall
12) Suez Canal
13) Wing Attack
14) River Murray
15) The Beatles
16) High Score
17) 1911
18) 1932
19) The Eiffel Tower
20) France
21) Pompeii
22) Animals
23) Russell
24) Four
25) Bells

Quiz Four

1. Who is the bear in The Jungle Book?
2. What is the female part of a flower called?
3. Sheriff Woody Pride and Buzz Lightyear are major characters in which series of films?
4. Which state of Australia has the biggest population?
5. Which animal is the symbol of the organisation known as the WWF?
6. Apart from the sticks, what do they use to play ice hockey with?
7. An elephant has only four teeth-True or False?
8. What was the name of the Kung Fu Panda in the film of that name?
9. What is both a name for a tornado and a floor game?
10. Which country has the highest population in the world?
11. In the bible, who built an ark?
12. When was decimal currency introduced in Australia?
13. Which teams have won the most VFL/AFL Premierships?
14. Which Australian city was attacked by Japanese midget submarines during World War Two?
15. What was the only farm machine the Ancient Romans had-a tractor, plough or thresher?
16. What is Lady Gaga's proper Christian name? Stacey, Sunny or Stefani?
17. What is the capital of Hawaii?
18. Which singing voice is the highest pitch? Soprano, tenor or baritone?
19. In which sport might you 'spike' and 'block'? Fencing, volleyball or golf?
20. Which language is spoken in Austria?
21. In what year was Gough Whitlam elected as Prime Minister of Australia-1971, 1972 or 1973?
22. What city does a Glaswegian live in?
23. What type of animal is Shrek's talkative best friend?
24. Not including jokers, how many cards are there in a standard deck of cards?
25. Recycling one aluminium can save enough energy to run a TV for three hours-True or False?

Answers

1) Baloo
2) Pistil
3) Toy Story
4) New South Wales
5) Panda
6) Puck
7) True
8) Po
9) Twister
10) China
11) Noah
12) 1966
13) Carlton and Essendon
14) Sydney
15) Plough
16) Stefani
17) Honolulu
18) Soprano
19) Volleyball
20) German
21) 1972
22) Glasgow
23) Donkey
24) 52
25) True

Quiz Five

1. Who painted the Mona Lisa?
2. If you were born on Christmas day, which star sign would you belong to?
3. What is the name of Donald Duck's girlfriend?
4. What is Australia's oldest political party?
5. Where were the first modern Olympic Games held?
6. In tennis what is the term used when the score is 40-40?
7. How many wives did King Henry Vlll of England have?
8. Which breed of dogs was menaced by Cruella de Vil?
9. What is the name of the mythical one horned, horse like creature?
10. What is the name of the river that runs through London?
11. In which number Century are we now living?
12. In which country in ancient times was mummification carried out on important people when they died?
13. What sport was Glenn McGrath famous in?
14. Which city houses the Royal Australian Mint?
15. What is the name of Will Smith's daughter, who is a singer?
16. What was Mickey Mouse's original name?
17. Which is the highest mountain in Africa?
18. Which U.S. President was Barack Obama? 43rd, 44th or 54th?
19. If a carnivore eats meat, what does a frugivore eat?
20. Where does the president of the United States of America live?
21. What structure divided Berlin in the years after World War ll?
22. How many strings do most violins have?
23. What did Babe the pig win a national title for-singing, shepherding or sty maintenance?
24. How long can a player hold on to a ball in netball?
25. In the film Bambi, what sort of animal is Flower?

Answers

1) Leonardo da Vinci
2) Capricorn
3) Daisy
4) Australian Labor Party
5) Greece-Athens
6) Deuce
7) Six
8) Dalmatians
9) Unicorn
10) River Thames
11) 21st
12) Ancient Egypt
13) Cricket
14) Canberra
15) Willow
16) Mortimer Mouse
17) Mount Kilimanjaro
18) 44th
19) A fruit eater
20) The White House
21) Berlin Wall
22) Four
23) Shepherding
24) Up to 3 seconds
25) Skunk

Quiz Six

1. Who lead a gang of outlaws in Sherwood Forest?
2. What is the second largest country in the world?
3. What is the name of the dog in Shaun the Sheep?
4. What animal is featured on the Australian 20c coin?
5. In which country would you find Mount Ararat?
6. In which sport would you perform a slam dunk?
7. The silver fern is the symbol for which national rugby team?
8. Which resident of Jellystone Park is "smarter than the average bear"?
9. What would you be lacking if you were an invertebrate?
10. How many countries make up the continent of South America-11, 12 or 14?
11. Complete the helpful memory aid: "I before E, except after . . .'?
12. What notable event affected London in September 1666?
13. In which city is Wembley a famous stadium?
14. What colour are seats in the Senate of the Australian Parliament?
15. What does the DC in Washington DC stand for?
16. What is the name of the actor who plays the character of Harry Potter in the movie series?
17. Which is the highest waterfall in the world?
18. What percentage of our body weight is water? 40%, 60% or 80%?
19. Which fingernail grows the fastest?
20. Which country does parmesan cheese come from?
21. Which member of Britain's Royal Family did Camilla Parker Bowles marry in 2005?
22. In art, acrylics and oils are types of what?
23. In the Wiggles, what colour skivvy does Anthony wear?
24. In which sport can you 'hang ten'?
25. What famous royal fortress holds England's crown jewels?

Answers

1) Robin Hood
2) Canada
3) Bitzer
4) Platypus
5) Turkey
6) Basketball
7) New Zealand
8) Yogi Bear
9) Backbone
10) 12
11) C
12) Great Fire of London
13) London
14) Red
15) District of Columbia
16) Daniel Radcliffe
17) Angel Waterfall
18) 60%
19) Middle finger
20) Italy
21) Prince Charles
22) Paint
23) Blue
24) Surfing
25) Tower of London

Quiz Seven

1. Who stole Christmas in a Dr Seuss book?
2. What is the biggest manmade structure on Earth?
3. Who fell in love with a robot called EVE?
4. What is the capital city of New South Wales?
5. Of which country is Teresa May the Prime Minister?
6. What is the board part of a skateboard called-plank, deck or block?
7. In which city would people ride in a gondola?
8. What is the name of the nanny played by Emma Thompson in two films?
9. In what country would you climb Mt Fuji?
10. Between which two counties is Niagara Falls?
11. Which occupation uses a trowel and spirit level?
12. What was signed by King John at Runnymede in 1215?
13. How many points are awarded for a win in a soccer match?
14. In what field of sport was Jack Brabham a world champion?
15. How many Dalmatian puppies were held captive in the film '101 Dalmatians'?
16. How many musicians constitute a big band?
17. Where was the sky city concept introduced for the first time?
18. Which is the only cat that can't retract its claws? Lion, puma or cheetah?
19. Where do the Canary Islands get their name from? Birds, dogs or lizards?
20. What is the most popular sport throughout the world?
21. In Ancient Rome which of these winged creatures was a good luck symbol-bee, eagle or owl?
22. In taekwondo, what is a dobok-kick, punch or uniform?
23. In the Toy Story films, what sort of doll is Woody?
24. Who were the first cheerleaders at an American football game-mothers of the players, children or men?
25. How many girls are in the Famous Five series of books?

Answers

1) The Grinch
2) Great Wall of China
3) WALL-E
4) Sydney
5) United Kingdom
6) Deck
7) Venice
8) Nanny McPhee
9) Japan
10) USA and Canada
11) Brick laying
12) Magna Cart
13) Three
14) Formula One Racing
15) 99
16) 10
17) Japan
18) The cheetah
19) From dogs- the canary bird is named after the islands
20) Football
21) Bee
22) Uniform
23) Cowboy
24) Men
25) Two

Quiz Eight

1. Sculptures of which animals lie at the base of Nelson's column?
2. What colour is a New York taxi?
3. Wolverine is the leader of which band of superheroes?
4. In which year did Parliament House open?
5. What nationality is the tennis player Roger Federer?
6. In what sport do they compete for the Ryder Cup?
7. In which US city is the Golden Gate Bridge?
8. For which film did Russell Crowe win the Best Actor Oscar?
9. What was red about the Red Baron, the WW1 flying ace-his beard, his plane or his flying suit?
10. What is the world's largest ocean?
11. In America they call it a sidewalk, what is it called in Australia?
12. For how many terms was Franklin D Roosevelt elected as US President?
13. What sport do the Green Bay Packers play?
14. What sea lies between Australia and New Zealand?
15. In cricket, how many runs equal a century?
16. Which Michael Jackson album spawned five chart-topping singles?
17. Which is the world's first national park?
18. Spell the word avocado.
19. In which country did 'Dubstep' dance music originate? USA, Brazil or England?
20. Global warming is caused by too much of which type of gas?
21. Sir Edmund Hillary was the first to climb what?
22. In Toy Story 2, what name is written on the bottom of Woody's boot?
23. What is the name of the cat that becomes Stuart's friend in Stuart Little 2-Snowball, Snowbell or Snowdrop?
24. What colour tennis clothes were players once required to wear?
25. Which planet has moons named Europa and Calisto?

Answers

1) Lions
2) Yellow
3) The X Men
4) 1988
5) Swiss
6) Golf
7) San Francisco
8) Gladiator
9) His plane
10) Pacific Ocean
11) Footpath
12) Four
13) Gridiron
14) Tasman Sea
15) 100
16) Bad
17) Yellowstone National Park USA
18) Avocado
19) England
20) Carbon Dioxide
21) Mt Everest
22) Andy
23) Snowball
24) White
25) Jupiter

Quiz Nine

1. What is the name of the Lion in The Lion, The Witch and the Wardrobe?
2. What is 75% of 200?
3. Which planet is known as "The Red Planet"?
4. In which Australian state or territory is Coober Pedy?
5. Which country's cricket team is named the Proteas?
6. What letter of the alphabet does a snowboard half pipe course look like- W, U or L?
7. Stamford Bridge is the home ground for which English soccer team?
8. Who was the youngest of the Beatles?
9. Which is the only piece of gymnastics equipment used by women- parallel bars, balance beam or rings?
10. What is the longest river in Europe- Volga, Danube or Rhine?
11. Who wrote the book Winnie the Pooh?
12. Before Queen Elizabeth, who held the record for longest serving British monarch?
13. In what country are the teams Real Madrid and Barcelona based?
14. What is the capital of Victoria?
15. Prior to adopting the euro, what was the currency of Italy?
16. Which Disney film does the 'Cheshire Cat' appear in?
17. What do you call a village that does not have a church?
18. Which are better adapted for living in salt water? Crocodiles or alligators?
19. Female hair grows quicker than male hair. True or False?
20. How many leaves does a shamrock have?
21. What was the first name of the French emperor with the surname Bonaparte?
22. When do your toenails grow fastest- winter, spring or summer?
23. Which Pixar film is set in Radiator Springs?
24. Which of these balls weighs the least- tennis ball, cricket ball or golf ball?
25. What country is associated with kilts and bagpipes?

Answers

1) Aslan
2) 150
3) Mars
4) South Australia
5) South Africa
6) U
7) Chelsea
8) George Harrison
9) Balance beam
10) Volga
11) A A Milne
12) Queen Victoria
13) Spain
14) Melbourne
15) Lira
16) Alice in Wonderland
17) A hamlet
18) Crocodiles
19) False
20) Three
21) Napoleon
22) Summer
23) Cars
24) Golf ball
25) Scotland

Quiz Ten

1. What was the name of Harry Potter's pet owl?
2. What is the world's largest rainforest called?
3. What term in mathematics refers to the number obtained when two or more numbers are multiplied?
4. Who has been Australia's most successful Olympian?
5. What country is the band U2 from?
6. In which sport is Billy Slater famous?
7. In which sport do you lunge, thrust and parry?
8. Which country has the Billboard charts to gauge record sales?
9. What flavour Campbell's soup did pop artist Andy Warhol usually paint?
10. How many territories are there as part of Australia-2, 5 or 10?
11. Ned Kelly was a famous outlaw in which country?
12. The name for which group of prehistoric animals comes from the Greek for "terrible lizard"?
13. What sport is Brett Favre famous for playing?
14. In what year of the 1980s did Advance Australia Fair become Australia's national anthem?
15. Who created the character Peter Rabbit?
16. n the fairy tale of Cinderella, what does Cinderella leave behind at the ball?
17. Which country is known as the roof of the world? Switzerland, Argentina or India?
18. Which sport uses the terms 'eagle' and 'albatross'?
19. What is the name of the Greek God of music?
20. Which continent is Thailand in?
21. In which country did reggae music originate?
22. What colour was the original Nintendo Wii game console?
23. What is the name of the princess in The Little Mermaid?
24. Who wears the heaviest equipment in any sport-baseball catcher, ice hockey goalie or cricketer?
25. Who is Winnie the Pooh's bounciest friend?

Answers

1) Hedwig
2) Amazon
3) The product
4) Ian Thorpe
5) Ireland
6) Rugby League
7) Fencing
8) USA
9) Tomato
10) 10
11) Australia
12) Dinosaur
13) Gridiron
14) 1984
15) Beatrix Potter
16) A glass slipper
17) Switzerland
18) Golf
19) Apollo
20) Asia
21) Jamaica
22) White
23) Ariel
24) Ice hockey goalie
25) Tigger

Quiz Eleven

1. Who is the son of Widow Twankey and brother of Wishee & Washee?
2. Which three colours make up the flag of Australia?
3. In computing, what is Mb short for?
4. What is the longest running Australian TV series of all time?
5. What is the main crop of China?
6. Who won the Brownlow Medal in AFL football in 2016?
7. What type of electricity makes hair stick to a comb or tumble dried clothes make a crackling sound?
8. Who wrote the children's books 'Charlie and the Chocolate Factory, The BFG, and Matilda'?
9. According to legend, what was the name of King Arthur's wizard friend?
10. What is the largest state of the USA?
11. Name the two planets closest to Earth?
12. Which team won the first VFL Premiership?
13. Which AFL teams has Gary Ablett Jnr played for?
14. In what Australian state or territory is Karratha?
15. October was originally what number month in the old Roman calendar?
16. Who released a song in 2014 called 'Lips are Movin'?
17. Which is the longest river in the world?
18. Which city is the Palace of Versailles nearest to?
19. What is the antonym of the word 'synonym'?
20. True or false: Antarctica is the coldest continent in the world?
21. Which of these fruits did Christopher Columbus discover in the New World-mango, date or pineapple?
22. What superhero does Mr Barney Krupp become when hypnotised?
23. What is Beyoncé's surname?
24. In 2010, John Isner and Nicholas Hahut played the longest match in history in which sport?
25. Which of these is not one of the primary colours-red, blue or green?

Answers

1) Aladdin
2) Red, white, blue
3) Megabyte
4) Four Corners
5) Rice
6) Patrick Dangerfield
7) Static electricity
8) Roald Dahl
9) Merlin
10) Alaska
11) Venus and Mars
12) Essendon
13) Geelong, Gold Coast Suns
14) Western Australia
15) Eighth
16) Meaghan Trainor
17) The Nile
18) Paris
19) Antonym
20) True
21) Pineapple
22) Captain Underpants
23) Knowles
24) Tennis
25) Green

Quiz Twelve

1. What is the artistic technique of gluing a number of items together to form a new work called?
2. What is a scalene triangle?
3. What colour are emeralds?
4. Which two Australian cities have hosted the summer Olympic Games?
5. Justin Trudeau is the Prime Minister of which country?
6. How many strikes would you need to score to get a perfect game in ten pin bowling?
7. Tug-o-war was once an Olympic event-True or False?
8. What colour are Mickey Mouse's shoes?
9. Which clouds are the highest-stratus, cumulus or cirrus?
10. What US city is the headquarters of the United Nations?
11. Which agency or organisation is responsible for the American space program?
12. Who has the highest batting average in Test cricket?
13. What three sports make up a triathlon?
14. What sport is Australian Greg Norman famous for playing?
15. What is a sea star more commonly known as?
16. What kind of creature was defeated by the Three Billy Goats Gruff?
17. Does a compass point towards the North or South Pole?
18. When was the first atomic bomb dropped?
19. What percentage of an egg's weight is the shell?
20. What country is the River Thames in?
21. In which year was the first Holden produced in Australia-1946, 1947 or 1948?
22. A marionette is a French song-True or False?
23. What superhero throws his boss through several walls and then asks, "I'm fired, aren't I"?
24. What boxer said he was the greatest because he could 'float like a butterfly and sting like a bee'?
25. At the top of every Scottish crest is a clan's what-sword, mascot or motto?

Answers

1) Collage
2) All sides are unequal
3) Green
4) Melbourne, Sydney
5) Canada
6) 12
7) True
8) Yellow
9) Cirrus
10) New York City
11) NASA
12) Don Bradman
13) Running, swimming, cycling
14) Golf
15) Starfish
16) A Troll
17) North Pole
18) August 6th 1945
19) 12%
20) England
21) 1948
22) False
23) Mr Incredible
24) Muhammad Ali (Cassius Clay)
25) Motto

Quiz Thirteen

1. Which artist painted a number of pictures of sunflowers?
2. Which ocean is located to the west of South America?
3. Which sport takes place in a velodrome?
4. What was the original name of Tasmania?
5. Which South American country is named after the Equator?
6. In which year of the 1980s did Australia win the America's Cup?
7. In which Australian state or territory is Devonport?
8. What is the largest brass instrument in an orchestra?
9. In which sport would you face a flipper or a doosra?
10. What created the Norwegian fjords- glaciers, volcanoes or earthquakes?
11. What word is missing at the end of this famous book title: 'The Lion, the Witch and the . . . ?
12. In what year did the Japanese first bomb Darwin during WWll?
13. What is the name of the Australian men's hockey team?
14. What animal is featured on the Australian 10c coin?
15. What kind of golf club do golfers normally use on the green to try and hit the ball into the hole?
16. Who has a dog called Snowy and is friends with Captain Haddock?
17. What is the largest continent in the world?
18. Which is the lowest point on the land of the United States continent?
19. Who said these words - 'I am the President of the United States and I am not going to eat any more broccoli'?
20. Which ocean separates North America from Europe?
21. In which city was the Colosseum built?
22. What is New Zealand's largest island-North Island, South Island or Stewart Island?
23. Which star of Twilight plays Jacob and is also a martial arts champion?
24. What is the highest number in a target area of a shuffleboard-6, 8 or 10?
25. What is the Southern Cross-a bridge, a star constellation or a tree?

Answers

1) Vincent van Gogh
2) Pacific
3) Cycling
4) Van Dieman's Land
5) Ecuador
6) 1983
7) Tasmania
8) Tuba
9) Cricket
10) Glaciers
11) Wardrobe
12) 1942
13) Kookaburras
14) (Superb) Lyrebird
15) Putter
16) Tintin
17) Asia
18) Death Valley California
19) George W Bush
20) Atlantic Ocean
21) Rome
22) South Island
23) Taylor Lautner
24) 10
25) Star constellation

Quiz Fourteen

1. What is the name of Peter Pan's piratical enemy?
2. If Sydney, Australia is 17 hours ahead of Chicago, America, what would the time be in Sydney is it is 1pm in Chicago?
3. From what country does Lego come?
4. Who was the first explorer to successfully cross Australia from top to bottom?
5. During which decade were the Beatles the most popular group in the world?
6. What do competitors push in a game of curling?
7. How many players are there in an Australian Rules football team on the field?
8. Which famous girl band did Cheryl Cole belong to?
9. What day of the week is considered a day of rest in Judaism?
10. What are the colours of the Japanese flag?
11. Which flower is associated with Remembrance Day in Britain?
12. For which team did Babe Ruth play for most of his career in baseball?
13. What do the letters NRL stand for?
14. In what year of the 1970s did colour television start in Australia?
15. In what continent is Germany?
16. Which television series is set in the town of Pontypandy?
17. In which country would you find the Eiffel Tower?
18. SLR is the abbreviation of what in the field of photography?
19. Which fruit was forbidden for Hawaiian women to eat by law?
20. True or false: The Empire State Building is the tallest building in America?
21. What was the first name of the scientist whose last name was Galilei?
22. In Finding Nemo, what occupation is the human that catches Nemo?
23. Which rap superstar was born Shawn Corey Carter?
24. What sport are the words birdie, putting and bunker linked to?
25. Which Leonardo da Vinci painting is famous for its smile?

Answers

1) Captain Hook
2) 6am
3) Denmark
4) John McDouall Stuart
5) 1960s
6) Stone
7) 18
8) Girls Aloud
9) Saturday
10) Red and white
11) Poppy
12) New York Yankees
13) National Rugby League
14) 1975
15) Europe
16) Fireman Sam
17) France
18) Single Lens Reflex camera
19) Coconut
20) False
21) Galileo
22) Dentist
23) Jay-Z
24) Golf
25) Mona Lisa

Quiz Fifteen

1. What did Romans use a hypocaust for?
2. What is the 11th letter of the alphabet?
3. What term in tenpin bowling describes having knocked all the pins down after your second bowl?
4. Where did the Federal Parliament meet before Canberra was established?
5. In which country was the first set of traffic lights installed?
6. How many players are there on a rugby union team?
7. What was discovered at Ballarat in the 1850s?
8. Who sang 'Everything has Changed' with Taylor Swift?
9. What colour is the skin of a polar bear?
10. The islands of Fiji are in the Atlantic Ocean-True or False?
11. What is American Buzz Aldrin famous for?
12. What famous structure was built on Salisbury Plain in the third millennium BC?
13. What position did Babe Ruth originally play in Major League baseball?
14. How many teams compete in the NRL competition?
15. What kind of creature is Manny from the 'Ice Age' films?
16. Which film and musical are about a miner's son who wishes to become a ballet dancer?
17. Which is the only US state that starts with the letter 'P'?
18. Which company is the largest producer of computer software for personal computers?
19. Why did the year 1994 see no baseball World Series?
20. Which country has an island called Sicily at its southern tip?
21. Which company released the Mackintosh computer in the 1980s?
22. What two colours would you mix to get turquoise?
23. What is Dora the Explorer's pet monkey named?
24. How many holes in most ten-pin bowling balls?
25. At Hogwarts, who became the High Inquisitor?

Answers

1) Heating their villas
2) K
3) Spare
4) Melbourne
5) England
6) 15
7) Gold
8) Ed Sheeran
9) Black
10) False-Pacific Ocean
11) Walking on the moon
12) Stonehenge
13) Pitcher
14) Sixteen
15) Woolly Mammoth
16) Billy Elliot
17) Pennsylvania
18) Microsoft
19) Player's strike
20) Italy
21) Apple
22) Blue and green
23) Boots
24) Three
25) Professor Delores Umbridge

Quiz Sixteen

1. What is the Canberra residence of the Australian Prime Minister called?
2. Which famous statue holds a torch in her right hand and is located in New York Harbour?
3. What is the capital city of Spain?
4. In what year did television commence in Australia?
5. What are the colours on the Irish flag?
6. What do the letters NBA stand for?
7. What language was spoken in Ancient Rome?
8. Who had a hit with a song called Uptown Funk?
9. In what town do the Simpsons live?
10. What is the largest country in the world, by area?
11. The Eiffel Tower is in which city?
12. In which country was Adolf Hitler born?
13. What sport is Karrie Webb famous for playing?
14. Who, so far, has been the only female Australian Prime Minister?
15. What force holds things to the Earth?
16. True or false? Harry Potter's middle name is James.
17. What is the largest island in the Mediterranean Sea?
18. Which was the first African country to qualify for a World Cup?
19. What is 'El Clásico'?
20. Name the imaginary line that runs around the Earth's surface the same distance between the North and South Poles?
21. The microwave was invented before the dishwasher-True or False?
22. What country in Europe would you visit to see the Black Forest?
23. Which US singer recorded the song OMG?
24. Badminton is an Olympic sport-True or False?
25. What is the more common name for the aurora borealis?

Answers

1) The Lodge
2) Statue of Liberty
3) Madrid
4) 1956
5) Green, white, orange
6) National Basketball Association
7) Latin
8) Mark Ronson (feat. Bruno Mars)
9) Springfield
10) Russia
11) Paris
12) Austria
13) Golf
14) Julia Gillard
15) Gravity
16) True
17) Sicily
18) Egypt 1934
19) Football match between Real Madrid and Barcelona
20) The Equator
21) False
22) Germany
23) Usher
24) True
25) Northern Lights

Quiz Seventeen

1. Which resident of Jellystone Park is "smarter than the average bear"?
2. How many of Snow White's seven dwarfs have names beginning with S?
3. Which sea separates Europe from Africa?
4. Which Australian city hosted the Commonwealth Games in 1962?
5. Prague is the capital of which European country?
6. What is the name of the Australian netball team?
7. Which building is located at 1600 Pennsylvania Ave. Washington DC?
8. In which Disney movie is a boy raised by a family of wolves?
9. In 2010, 33 miners were trapped in a mine for 69 days in which South American country-Brazil, Peru or Chile?
10. What is the capital city of Italy?
11. What type of fruit is dried to make raisins?
12. What is Alcatraz famous for?
13. How many Olympic gold medals has Usain Bolt won in total?
14. Which notorious Australian's last words were 'Such is life'?
15. What famous monster reptile is known as Gojira in Japan?
16. Who had a hit in 2008 with 'Single Ladies (Put a Ring on it)'?
17. What is the largest Scandinavian country?
18. How many cricket World Cups have been won by Australia?
19. Which basketball team is as well-known for their comic antics as for their on-court skills?
20. Which island country lies off China, Korea and Russia?
21. What wooden animal did the Greeks hide in to capture the city of Troy?
22. What's the most popular engine to take orders from Sir Topham Hat?
23. Who had a hit with Someone That I Used to Know?
24. What do boxers wear on their hands underneath their gloves?
25. What did the Salem trials accuse people of being-giants, witches or spies?

Answers

1) Yogi Bear
2) Two-Sleepy, Sneezy
3) Mediterranean Sea
4) Perth
5) Czech Republic
6) Diamonds
7) The White House
8) The Jungle Book
9) Chile
10) Rome
11) Grapes
12) A prison
13) Eight
14) Ned Kelly
15) Godzilla
16) Beyoncé
17) Sweden
18) Five
19) Harlem Globetrotters
20) Japan
21) Horse
22) Thomas the Tank Engine
23) Gotye
24) Bandages
25) Witches

Quiz Eighteen

1. How many sides does a hexagon have?
2. Which of the following countries is not in Europe: Spain, Greece, Egypt or Belgium?
3. Which desert covers much of northern Africa?
4. What is the largest desert in Australia?
5. Which continent almost doubles in size during winter?
6. Which two Australian cities have hosted the Formula One Grand Prix?
7. Daffy and Donald are what type of animal?
8. In the 12 Days of Christmas song, what type of bird is sitting in a pear tree?
9. Which is further south, Adelaide or Perth?
10. In which country is the city of Barcelona?
11. How many months of the year have 31 days?
12. Which teams have won the most FA Cups?
13. In what year of the 1970s did Australia compete in its first World Cup of football?
14. How many Academy Awards has Cate Blanchett won?
15. Who is Gregory's best friend in the 'Diary of a Wimpy Kid' books?
16. Who wrote Willy Wonka and the Chocolate Factory?
17. In which Australian state would you find Kalgoorlie?
18. In cross-country bike racing, what do the initials BMX represent?
19. What is the maximum time limit allowed to look for a lost ball in golf?
20. What are the only two countries to have a land border with the US?
21. In what year of the 1970s did Elvis Presley die?
22. Which of the Seven Dwarfs has the longest beard?
23. What kind of animal is Santa's Little Helper in The Simpsons?
24. What mark does a bowler put on a scoresheet to indicate a strike?
25. Which African river flows into the Victoria Falls-Zambezi, Congo or Nile?

Answers

1) Six
2) Egypt
3) Sahara Desert
4) Great Victoria Desert
5) Antarctica
6) Adelaide, Melbourne
7) Duck
8) Partridge
9) Adelaide
10) Spain
11) Seven
12) Arsenal, Manchester United
13) 1974
14) Two
15) Rowley
16) Roald Dahl
17) Western Australia
18) Bicycle Moto X (Cross)
19) 5 minutes
20) Canada and Mexico
21) 1977
22) Sleepy
23) Dog
24) An X
25) Zambezi

Quiz Nineteen

1. Which is the only vowel not on the top row of a computer keyboard?
2. True or false: the biggest bone in the human body is located in your leg?
3. What sort of animal is the video game character Sonic?
4. How many kangaroos are there on the Australian $1 coin?
5. What are Caribbean steel drums traditionally made of-old cars, oil drums or tyre rims?
6. What is the most popular sport in the Netherlands-football, swimming or running?
7. How long did Phileas Fogg take to go around the world?
8. Harry Potter went to which school?
9. What swordsman leaves the mark of Z?
10. What is Australia's largest city?
11. What is the capital city of Russia?
12. On what date is Remembrance Day?
13. In what country is the Wanderers Cricket Ground?
14. Which river runs through the city of Melbourne?
15. The company Oakley Inc. is best known for producing what type of clothing accessory?
16. What was the name of Dorothy's dog in the Wizard of Oz?
17. What two colours make up the flag of Spain?
18. Who developed the World Wide Web {www} Tim Berners Lee, Charles Babbage or Jim Osborne?
19. How many feathers are used to make badminton shuttle- a. 10 to 12 b. 18 to 20 c. 14 to 16?
20. What letter do cars from Germany have on them when travelling abroad to show what country they come from?
21. There were no female pharaohs in Ancient Egypt-True or False?
22. What are both a Greek mythological woman and a popular charm bracelet?
23. Lightning McQueen uses Goodyear tyres in Cars-True or False?
24. What's the most common injury for a learner snowboarder- dislocated shoulder, wrist sprain or broken foot?
25. Which chocolate treat were invented first-hot chocolate, chocolate bars or cake?

Answers

1) E
2) True-the femur
3) A hedgehog
4) Five
5) Oil drums
6) Football
7) 80 days
8) Hogwarts
9) Zorro
10) Sydney
11) Moscow
12) November 11th
13) South Africa
14) Yarra River
15) Sunglasses
16) Toto
17) Red and yellow
18) Tim Berners Lee
19) 14 to 16
20) D
21) False
22) Pandora
23) False
24) Wrist sprain
25) Hot chocolate

Quiz Twenty

1. What is the innermost colour of a rainbow?
2. When added together, how many days are there in the months of October, November and December?
3. How many players are there in a baseball team?
4. How many teams make up the Australian AFL competition?
5. In which ocean is the Mariana Trench, the deepest point in the Earth's surface?
6. In which sport is Eli Manning a famous player?
7. Wood from what tree is used to make cricket bats?
8. Which famous girl band released a song called 'Black Magic' in 2015?
9. What gas can be put in tubes to make colourful, bright signs?
10. What is the world's smallest ocean?
11. Which male singer had hit songs in 2016 with 'Sorry' and 'Love Yourself'?
12. In what year did the first man walk on the moon?
13. At how many Olympics did Dawn Fraser represent Australia?
14. What were the Australian states known as before Federation?
15. What is the main ingredient in an omelette, quiche and frittata?
16. What nationality is the singer Sia?
17. In which country is Mount Everest located?
18. Which sporting great was dubbed 'The Boy from Bowral'?
19. Which is the biggest flower in the world-Rafflesia, Wolfia or Sunflower?
20. In which country is the Eyjafjallajökull volcano, whose eruption affected air flights in 2010?
21. How many years was Nelson Mandela in prison-25, 27 or 29 years?
22. What body part do crickets use to chirp?
23. In what field of the arts are Grammy Awards presented?
24. What's the most common injury for a learner snowboarder-dislocated shoulder, wrist sprain or broken foot?
25. What tablet computer did Apple release in 2010?

Answers

1) Violet
2) 92 days
3) Nine
4) 18
5) Pacific Ocean
6) Gridiron
7) Willow
8) Little Mix
9) Neon
10) Arctic Ocean
11) Justin Bieber
12) 1969
13) Three
14) Colonies
15) Eggs
16) Australian
17) Nepal
18) Sir Donald Bradman
19) Rafflesia
20) Iceland
21) 27
22) Legs
23) Music
24) Yellow
25) iPad

Quiz Answer Page

Name: _____

1. _____
2. _____
3. _____
4. _____
5. _____
6. _____
7. _____
8. _____
9. _____
10. _____
11. _____
12. _____
13. _____
14. _____
15. _____
16. _____
17. _____
18. _____
19. _____
20. _____
21. _____
22. _____
23. _____
24. _____
25. _____

Total Score: _____

Quiz Answer Page

Team Name: _____

1. _____
2. _____
3. _____
4. _____
5. _____
6. _____
7. _____
8. _____
9. _____
10. _____
11. _____
12. _____
13. _____
14. _____
15. _____
16. _____
17. _____
18. _____
19. _____
20. _____
21. _____
22. _____
23. _____
24. _____
25. _____

Total Score: _____

Printed in Great Britain
by Amazon